ABC
SCHOOL

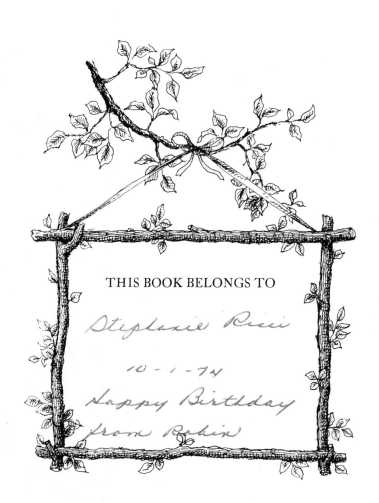

THIS BOOK BELONGS TO

Stephanie Ricci

10-1-74

Happy Birthday

from Robin

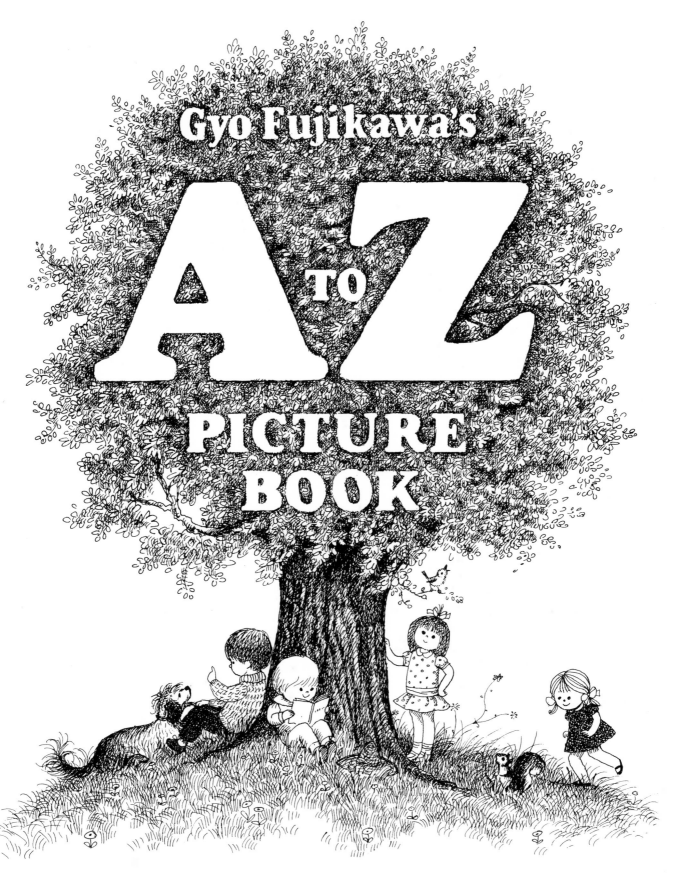

Gyo Fujikawa's A TO Z PICTURE BOOK

GROSSET & DUNLAP · PUBLISHERS · NEW YORK

Books with pictures by
Gyo Fujikawa

A CHILD'S GARDEN OF VERSES
THE NIGHT BEFORE CHRISTMAS
BABIES
BABY ANIMALS
MOTHER GOOSE
A CHILD'S BOOK OF POEMS
FAIRY TALES AND FABLES

Library of Congress Catalog Card Number: 73-16655
ISBN: 0-448-11741-X   (Trade Edition)
ISBN: 0-448-13205-2   (Library Edition)

Acorn

Alligator

Anchor

Amaryllis

Automobile

Airplane

Artist

Argument

Anger

Agreement

Eat an apple going to bed—
make the doctor beg his bread.

Armadillo

A is for alone,
all by myself . . .
Hi, there, frog!
Can I play with you?

Bobolink

Bashful

Bugle

Butterfly

Ball

Bow

Bonnet

Bunny

Bib

Bottle

Bear

Bell

Black eye

Banana

Boat

Boots

Blackberries

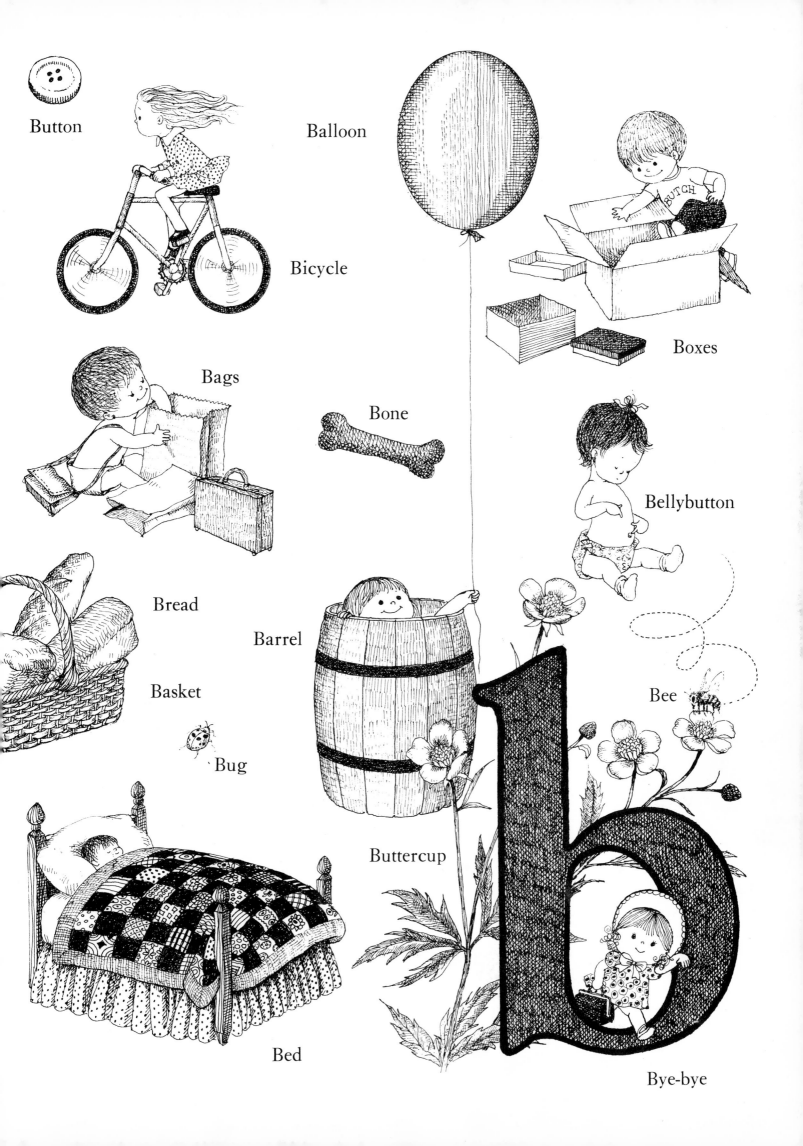

Button

Balloon

Bicycle

Boxes

Bags

Bone

Bellybutton

Bread

Barrel

Bee

Basket

Bug

Buttercup

Bed

Bye-bye

B is for busy babies!

Clover

Candy

Chipmunk

Clown

Cone

Chicken

Chicks

Cow

Crown

Chocolate Cake

Calf

Chair

Cuckoo Clock

Chickadee

Charlie is Cold

Clara is Crawling

Camel

Cat and Copy Cat

Crybaby

Crab

Cactus

Cheese

Caterpillar

C is for city!

Daisy

Dormouse

Deer

Dragonfly

Doctor

Doll

Dogs

Dachshund

Duck and Ducklings

Dove

Diver

Dolphin

David Digs

Daffodil

Doghouse

Dandelion

D is for dreams,
    all kinds of dreams,

dangerous . . .   and delicious ones . . .

dreadful . . .　　　　delightful . . .　　　　and disgusting ones!

Edelweiss

Emma cleans
her Ears

Eye

Elephant

Elf

Eskimo

Edward is Eating

Eggs

Frog

Fox

Furry Friends

Figleaf

Fig

Fishes

Feather

Flamingo

Forget-me-not

Fearless Freddie

F is for
   friends,
   fairies,
   flowers,
   fishes,
   and frogs.

Gossip

Gull

Grapes

Giraffe

Geranium

Goose

May the
Garland
of friendship
be ever
Green

Ginny
is a
Giggler

Hummingbird

Halo

Harp

Hatchet

Hammer

House

Home Sweet Home

Hollyhocks

Horse

h

Henry is Hungry
for his

Harold is Happy
with his

Hamburger

Hot dog

H is for Halloween!

Icebergs

Iron

Igloo

Icing

Ibis

Iris

Ice Cream

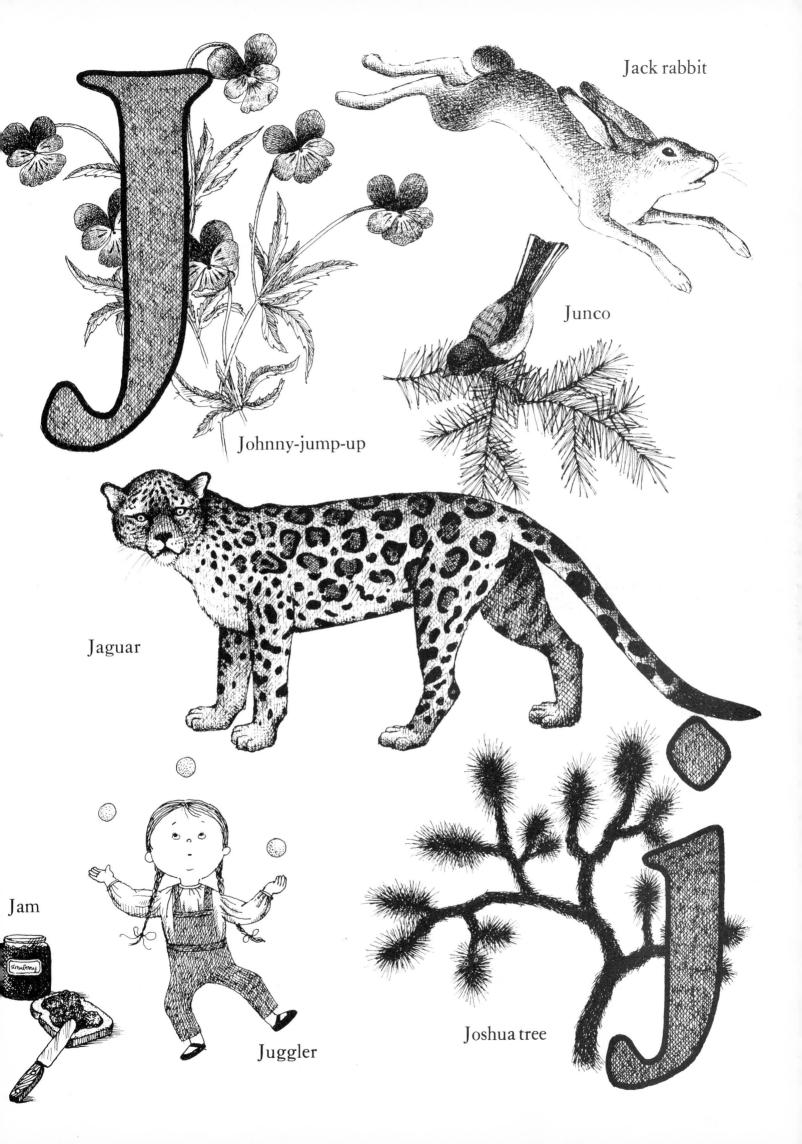

Jack rabbit

Junco

Johnny-jump-up

Jaguar

Jam

Juggler

Joshua tree

J is for
jump,
jump,
jump!

Kookaburra

Katydid

Kenny is
kowtowing.

Kangaroo

Koala

Key

Kiwi

k

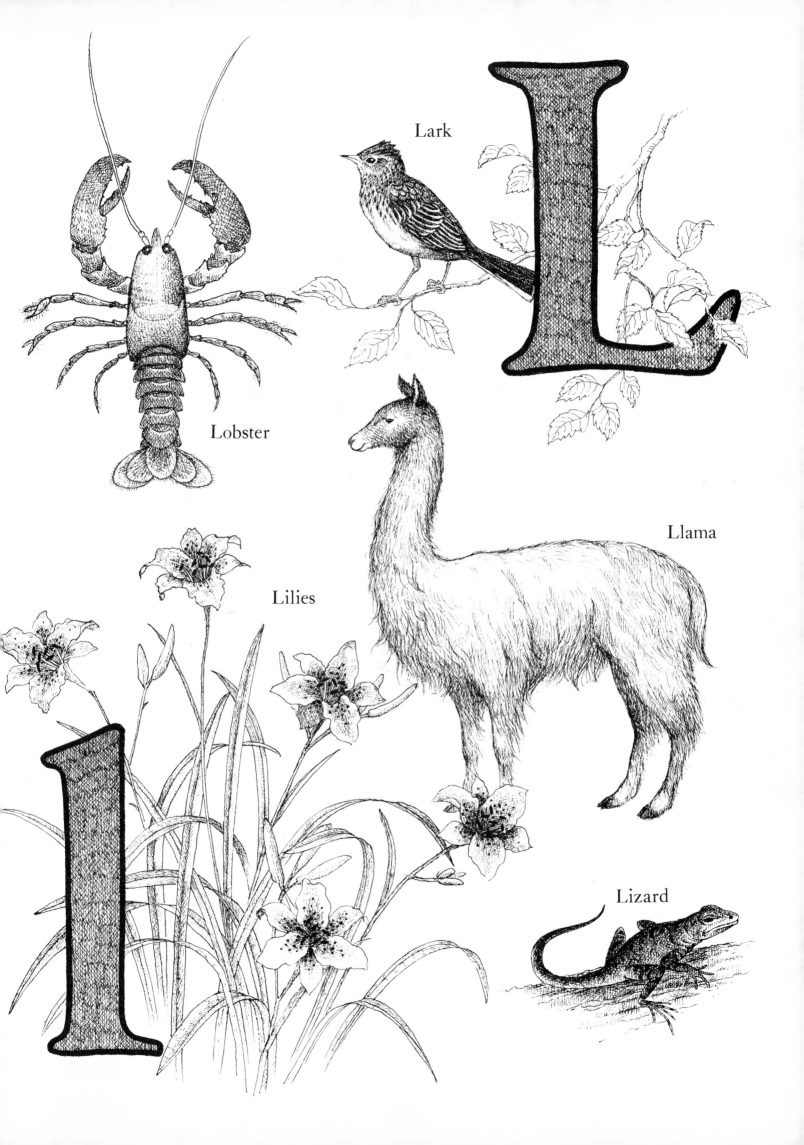

Lark

Lobster

Lilies

Llama

Lizard

L is for lullaby,
    lions,
    lizards,
    lemons,
    and lambs.

L is for love,
    leopard,
    and lilies of the valley.

Moon

Mountains

Mulberry

Mouse

Monkey

Mint

Melon

Meow

Mitten

Muffler

Muff

Morning-glory

Moo goo gai pan

Mockingbird

Mackerel

Moose

Marigold

Milk

Mushrooms

m

M is for
    my mean
    and marvelous
    monsters.

Nest

Newt

Nene

Nasturtium

Nurse

Nautilus

Necklace

Nightingale

Nuts

Nestlings

N is for numbers!

Owl

Ostrich

Orange

Octopus

Opossum

Otter

Orchid

Onions

Plum pudding

Parrot

Pumpkin pie

Pig

Potato

Pear

Peach

Panda

Peter pouts

Puppy

Pansies

P is for
pigeon,
penguin,
peacock,
puddle
and polliwogs.

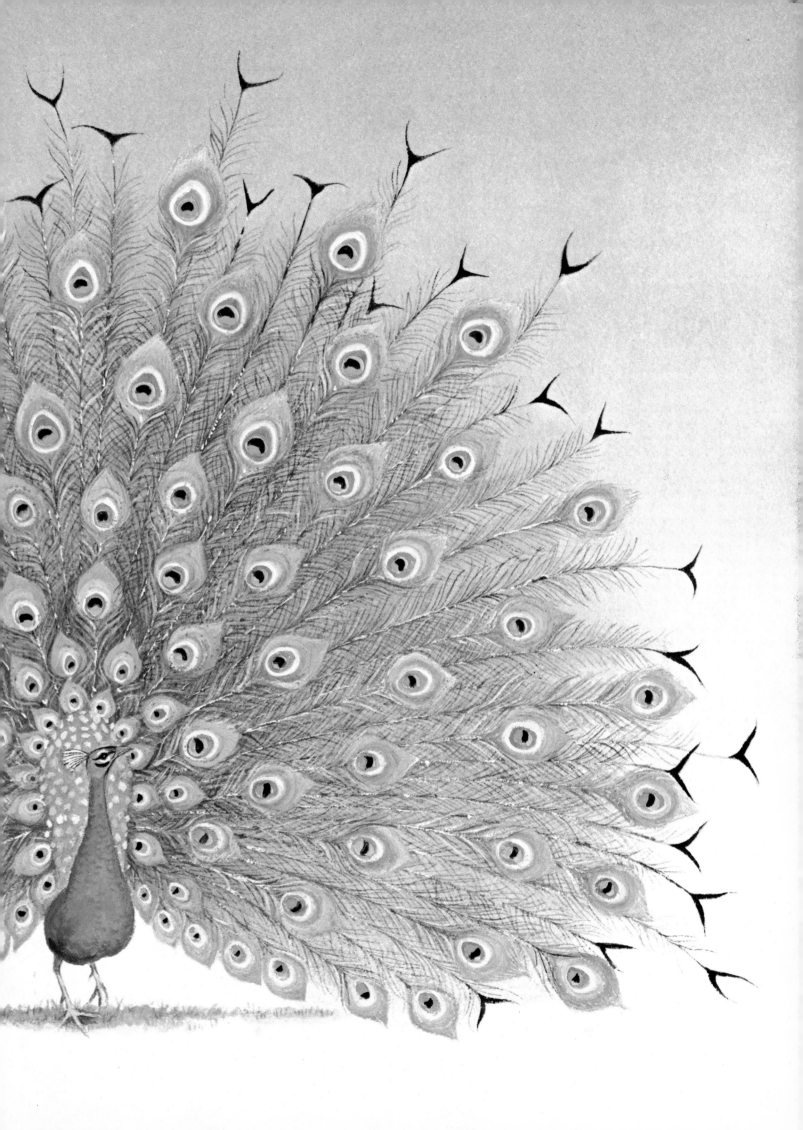

Queue

Queen

Quail

Quiet!

Queen Anne's lace

Quarrel

Quill

Quintuplets

Robin

Rose

Raccoon

Rhinoceros

Rolling pin

Raspberries

Rat

R is for rain, rain,
    and lots more rain.
Stop! I say—
Enough is enough!

Shower

Swallow

Starfish

Sponge

Soap

Smiling Sam swims

Sandpiper

Snake

Stuck-up

Seal

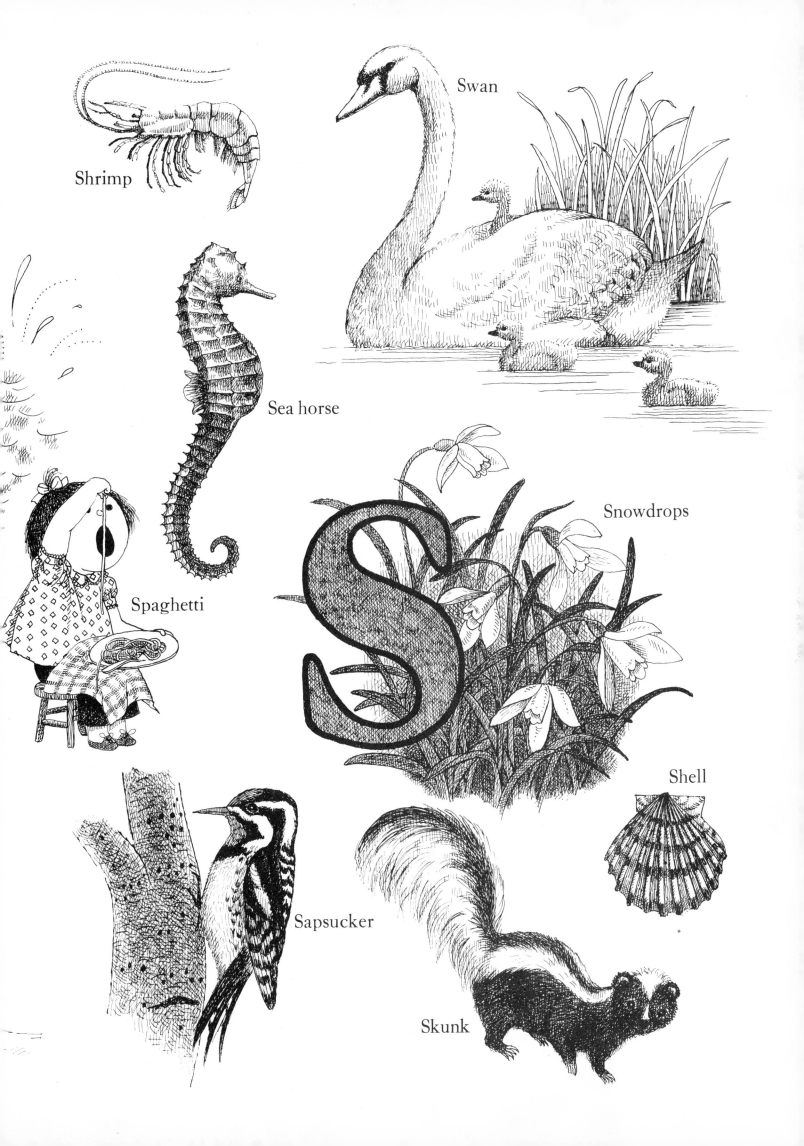

Shrimp

Swan

Sea horse

Spaghetti

Snowdrops

S

Shell

Sapsucker

Skunk

S is for sunflowers,
squirrels,
strawberries,
and snails.

S is for black-eyed Susans,
and spiders,
and Sam the setter.

S is for summertime,
sparrows,
and snoozes
in secret shelters.

Teardrops

Thimble

Tiger lily

Thrasher

Teeth

Toothbrush

Toothpaste

Towel

Toboggan

Tabby

Tall

Tramp

Tomato

Tough   Tender

Thanksgiving turkey

Thyme

Tough   Tender

Toad

t

Tugboat

Trumpet

Trout

T is for
topsy-turvy!

Tiger

Trees

Tepee

Taxicab

Tulips

Triplets

Thistles

Tightrope

Train

Trapeze

Tuba

Tow truck

Teddy bear

Teapot

Toucan

Teacup

Turtle

Up

Under

Ugly

Umbrella

Unicorn

Urn

Upside-down cake

Ukulele

Unhappy

Vain

Vane

Visit

Volcano

Vaccination

Be My Valentine

Valise

Violet

Vest

Violin

V is for
vegetables.

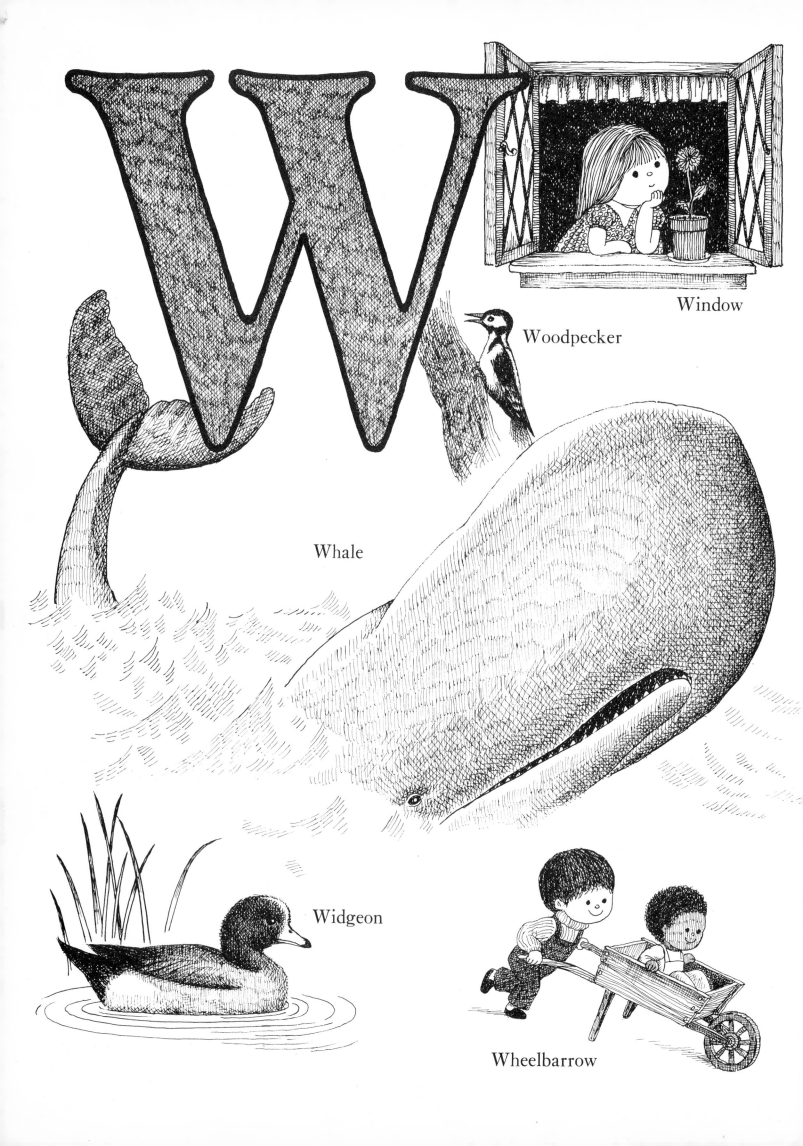

Window

Woodpecker

Whale

Widgeon

Wheelbarrow

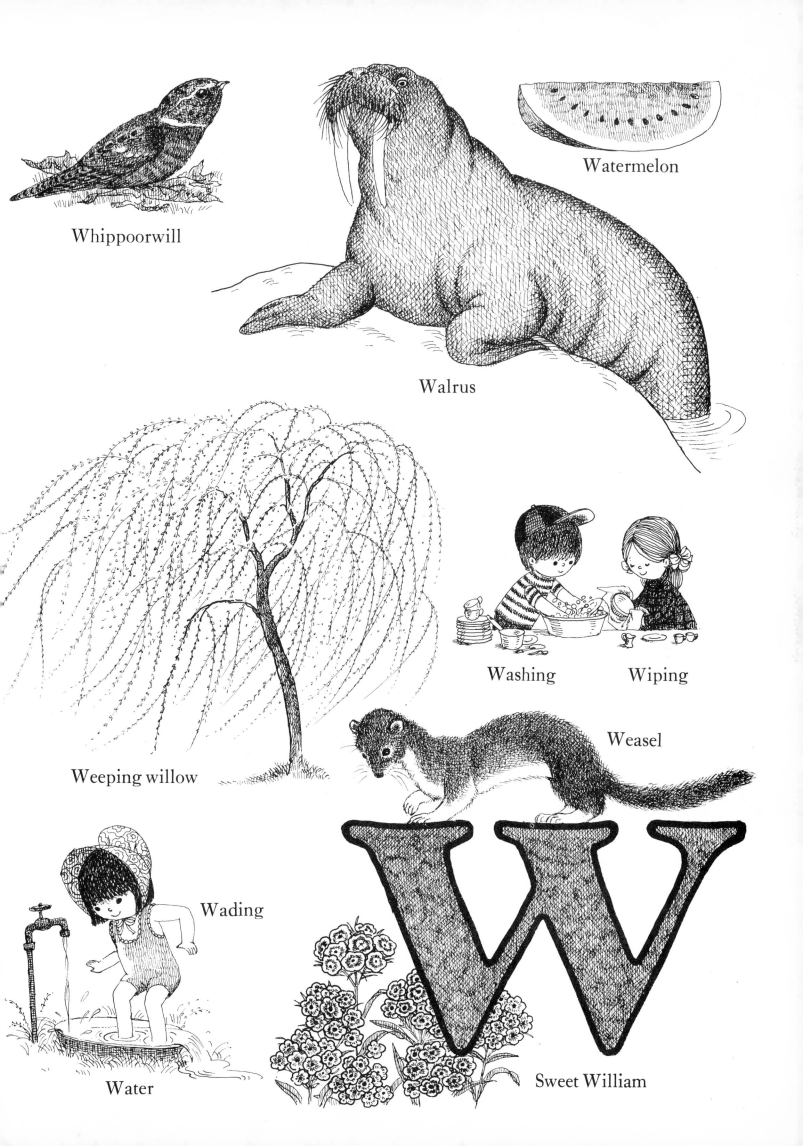

Whippoorwill

Walrus

Watermelon

Weeping willow

Washing   Wiping

Weasel

Wading

Water

Sweet William

W is for long wintertimes,
    the whistling wind,
    the winter wren,
    and the worm.

W is for the woodchuck, too,
    warm and nestled in his bed.
    How wise to sleep away the time
    until the welcome spring!

X-ray

X marks the spot.

XXXXXX is for kisses.

X is for
railroad crossing.

Xeranthemum

Xylophone

Yak

Yoo-hoo!

Yew

Yellow jacket

Yo-yo

Yacht

Yam

Yawn

Yucca

Y is for
    yuletide!

Zinnia

Zombie

Zero

Zipper